What needs to be broken before it can be used?

An egg.

D1516916

Who is the Easter Bunny's favorite actor?

Anthony HOPkins.

Why should Easter eggs beware of good jokes?

They may crack up!

What did one jelly bean say to other?

You're a real sweetie!

Which is the best place to buy some ham?

Hamazon.

Why did all the Easter eggs look so tired?

Because they were egg-zosted.

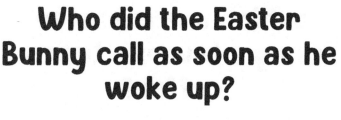

Who did the Easter Bunny call as soon as he woke up?

His hare dresser.

Which train takes you to the best Easter party in town?

Easter eggs-press.

Why couldn't the Easter Bunny become an actor?

He was eggs-pressionless.

Which one is Easter Bunny's favorite type of coffee?

Eggs-presso!

What gets the Easter Bunny moving?

Hip-Hop music.

Which is the Easter Bunny's favorite show?

The Kardashi-hens.

How do pigs show love and support to each other?

By holding each others hamds.

How did the Easter Bunny get so fat?

Because he doesn't eggs-ercise.

Why did the Easter Bunny's car not go anywhere?

Because he forgot to eggs-elerate.

Who did the Easter
Bunny meet at the flea
market?

Bugs Bunny.

How do you make Easter
easier?

You replace the t with
an i.

Why did the Easter
Bunny reject the Easter
eggs?

Because they were all
beaten-up!

What is a jelly bean's favorite kind of music?

Beanie-weenie ballads.

What did the bunnies and eggs have in common?

They had no hambition in life.

Which is the Easter Bunny's favorite day to have eggs?

Fry-day!

How is the Easter chick so smart?

He reads the hen-cyclopedia.

How did Ms. Piggy like her eggs?

Cadbury Creme Eggs.

Why are eggs laid?

Because dropping eggs would break them.

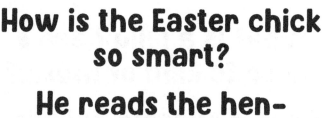

Why was there a jam session on Easter?

Because the jelly beans banded to sing together.

What were the angry potato's words during the fight?

You better be careful, or I'll mash you!

What do you call an Easter Bunny who loves his Easter eggs too much?

Easter egg-centric

Why nobunny asked for cupcakes?

Because those are just flamboyant muffins!

What kind of cakes do bunnies care the most about?

Carrot cakes.

What do you see at the end of Easter?

Letter r.

Why did the Chocolate Bunny see a therapist?

Because he felt hollow inside.

How can you say that Mr. Pig failed as an Easter Bunny?

By the egg on its face.

What was Bunny's eggcellent idea for a balanced diet?

One cupcake in each hand.

What did the Easter Bunny buy for Mrs. Bunny?

A 24-carrot gold ring.

Why did the pig become an actor?

Because he was eggcellent at hamming it up!

What did Mr. Pig say to Ms. Piggy when she was leaving angrily?

I am bacon you to stay, please.

Why was Little Easter Bunny praised at school?

Because she egg-selled in all the subjects.

How did the Easter story book end?

All the characters lived HOPPILY ever after.

Which is Ms. Piggy's favorite Ballet?

Swine Lake.

Do potatoes like bribes?

Absolutely. They enjoy some buttering-up.

What did the Easter Bunny buy online?

Many hare products.

Why couldn't the bunny pronounce shopping?

Because it was hopping

What is Bunny's aviation fleet called?

Hare Force

What do pigs use to tie things together?

Hamstrings.

Is butchering the puns okay?

Nope. A big misteak.

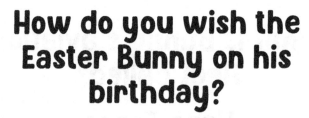

How do you wish the Easter Bunny on his birthday?

You say hoppy birthday

Would February March?

No, but April May.

What did Ms. Piggy say when she saw Mr. Pig at the party?

"Hamn! You clean up well"

What do piglets listen to before going to sleep?

Piggy tales.

What makes one Easter bunny flirt with the other?

The ear-resistibility.

What did the Easter Bunny find at the retail store?

A new tail!

Why is the Easter Bunny's skin so healthy?

He eggs-foliate

Why was the Easter Bunny so quiet and aloof at the party?

He was having an egg-sistential crisis.

Why was the Easter party planned at the beach?

Because there was a beach-hatch.

What do you call a jellybean that is dressed up?

A bean in a tuxedo.

Where did the Easter Bunny study medicine?

At John HOPkins.

The rabbit who cracks jokes is called?

A funny bunny.

Which is Jelly Bean's favorite dance?

The jolly dance.

What kind of stories do eggs tell their kids at night?

Yolk tales.

What is Easter eggs' favorite fun activity at parties?

Karayolke.

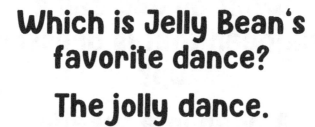

Can a pig become a
successful actor?

He sure has a chance to
make great acting
chops.

What did kid bunnies
play at the park?

HOPscotch

Who protects the Easter
bunny?

A bunny guard.

Why did the carrots go to the haredresser?

Because its roots were showing.

Name a city famous for hatching eggs. Chick-ago.

Knock! Knock! Who's there? LettuceLettuce, who? Lettuce in and you will know.

What did the Rainbow Cauliflower say to the Easter Egg Radish? You look absolutely radishing!

How did the Easter Bunny feel after he met Mr. Carrot? He was delighted to gnaw him.

Who did Easter Bunny call when he faced a pest problem at the farm? The eggs-terminators

How good is the Easter Bunny at basketball? He is world-famous for his baskets.

What is a bunny with no hair called? Hareless.

How do you know the age of a rabbit? You check the gray hares.

Where did Mr. and Mrs. Bunny go after their wedding? On their Bunnymoon.

What is a bunny with an onion called? A bunion.

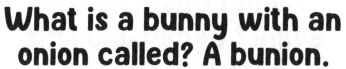

Where was the Brown Bunny at the Easter party? He arrived choco-late.

What did the pig say after feasting on the pork chops? "I am quite stuffed."

Why was Mr. Comedian Bunny upset at the event? Because all his best yolks were poached.

Why were all the bunnies shocked at the movie screening? Because the film was hare-raising.

How do you show your
love to Baby Eggs? By
adding some egg-stra
cheese to their food.

 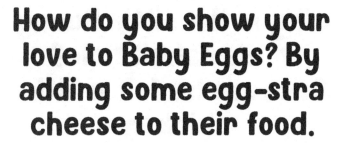

One product bunnies
can't go out without?
Hare-spray.

What did Mrs. Bunny
say? That she was
hopping to see her kids
this Easter.

Why is the Little Bunny
in his rabbit hole?
Because he felt a little
chicken.

Why was Mr. Chocolate
Bunny dark? Because he
felt a little bitter.

Where do bunnies find
love? In a HOPless place.

How can we make Mr. Choco Bunny feel better? Bitter to better is an acquired taste that comes with time.

Where did the Cute Bunny hide all her candies? In her stomach.

What did Mr. Duck wear to the party? A ducksedo.

How did the chicken
taste? Eggs-quisite.

Was Mr. Bunny attentive
when you told him the
Easter joke? He was all
ears.

Why did the chocolate
bar have a toothache?
There was a chip in its
tooth.

What did the Easter
bunny wear before
going off for a run?
Snickers.

What do you get if you
mix ducks with
fireworks?
Firequackers.

How did the baby eggs
steal chocolates from
the store? They first
choc-ed out a plant and
then egg-secuted it.

What is brown and not made of chocolate? A cocoa-not!

How was the first experience of eating mint chocolates for the bunny? It was enjoy-mint.

Which candy is super rich and happy?

Bounty-ful?

How did Easter end?
With an r.

Why were the eggs on a journey? They were on a mission to eggs-plore the world.

How much did Easter Bunny make for making a basket? He made two points, like rest of the players.

What kind of jokes to
eggs tell? Egg yolks!

Why did the donut go to
the dentist? It wanted a
chocolate filling.

Why didn't the bunny
hop? No bunny knows
the answer.

What do you get when you cross beer with a chocolate bar? A Choco-Light!

A bunny with a large head is more commonly called what? An egg-head.

How did Easter end? On a hoppy note.

What chocolate bar never laughs at jokes? The one that chooses to only Snickers.

Which is a chocoholic's favorite kind of party? One that's choco-lit!

Which candy is never on time? ChocoLATE

Why do eggs hate being tickled? They are afraid to crack-up!

What is the Easter Bunny's favorite seat? The eggs-it row!

What blossoms between your nose and chin? Tulips

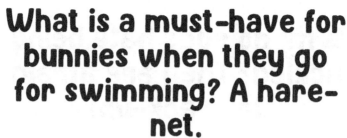

What is a must-have for bunnies when they go for swimming? A hare-net.

Which season is trampoline season? Spring season!

Why was the porkchop single? Because he was waiting to meat his match.

How do you know A is full of sweet fragrances? Because B comes after it.

What eggs-ercise do bunnies prefer to stay in shape? Hareobics.

What keeps the bunny's hair neat? A hare brush.

What makes a rabbit
stew? Being made to
wait for hours.

How did the rooster flirt
with the hen he found
attractive? He said,
"You're one hot chick!"

"What's for lunch?" the
duck asked. "Soap and
quackers," the cook
replied.

What advice were the blue bunnies given? To cheer up!

What does a bunny do with a pair of socks? Sock hop.

What is a bunny with a dictionary in his pocket called? A smarty pant.

Which duck plays basketball?

Slam duck.

How is the Easter Bunny so good with the horse? Because he learned to groom and hare-ness the horse.

How come the jelly bean won three races at a stretch? It was on a roll!

What was Easter Bunny's reaction when he was paid less than eggspected? Yolk got to be kidding me!

Why was dark chocolate all over the place? Because the chocolate Bunny melted with all the love it got showered with.

Recommend a horror film for chicks to watch on Easter. The eggsorcism of Easily Roast.

Why are the students studying so hard during their Easter break? For their spring eggsams

What is the one rule before Egg hunting season? No poaching is allowed.

How does one leave an Easter party? By making a classic eggs-it.

Recommend a book to read over the Easter break. Great eggs-pectations by Charles Chicken.

How should you go about an Easter hunt? You must ask an eggs-pert first.

Why did Mr. Bunny ask for more and more chocolate eggs? Because he couldn't get an oeuf.

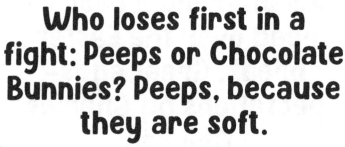

Who loses first in a fight: Peeps or Chocolate Bunnies? Peeps, because they are soft.

What did one egg say to the other? I hope your dye job is going well?

When do you place all your eggs in one basket? On Easter.

Why did baby chick
cross the road alone?
Because all her Peeps
were on the other side.

It takes how many eggs
to change an empty
basket? Just one, as the
basket no longer
remains empty.

Which branch of
military recruits the
most rabbits? Hare-
force.

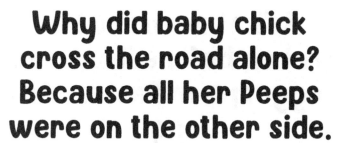

What needs to be broken before it is used, eggcept on Easter. An egg.

What is a colony of rabbits marching in a straight line called? A hareline.

Which oyster treats are found at the bottom of the ocean? Oyster eggs.

Why were all the other bunnies jealous of the Comedian Bunny? Because he was the only funny bunny.

What do bunny lovers say to each other? I'd hop to the moon and back for you.

What did the bunny say as he left the party angrily? I don't carrot about this treat anymore.

Why are too many egg puns not good? They stop being bunny.

How do you flirt with a bunny? You call them hop stuff.

What do you say when you see a sad bunny? Don't, bunny. Be hoppy!

Which is Easter Bunny's
favorite Queen song?
Some Bunny to love...

Why was the Easter
dance marathon such a
huge success? Everyone
hip-hopped, and didn't
stop!

What should you do
when you run out of
chocolate Easter
candies? You must give
other Peeps a chance.

How do you have so much Easter dinner leftover? You must have really hammed it up!

How good was the Easter meal that the Bunny Family prepared? It was to dye for!

Why were the chicken eggstra chirpy on Easter? They were eggsited.

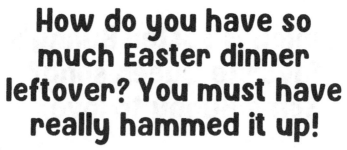

What did Mrs. Hen say when she found great Easter treats? Chick out these amazing gifts!

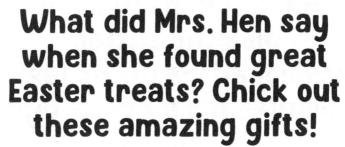

What do you say when you call your family on Easter? Happy Easter to my Peeps!

What's a pig family called? A ham-fam!

What happens when you plan the Easter celebrations at the last minute? It's a do-or-dye situation.

What did Mr. Bunny say when everyone arrived for the Easter party? Ears to a good Easter!

Why should we not cross an Easter Bunny with a stressed person? To avoid getting a basket case.

Why did the bunnies
watch Avengers:
Endgame on Easter?
Because it had Rabbit
Downey Jr.

Why are eggs painted?
Because it is easier than
wallpapering them.

What kind of plants do
eggs grow? Eggplant?

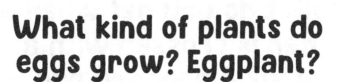

What happened to the egg-mobile after the lights turned green? It eggs-elerated.

Why couldn't the Easter Egg Family switch on their TV? Because it was scrambled.

What do you get when a hen is crossed with a dog? A pooched egg.

What makes people tired in April? The end of a March.

Why was the Easter Bunny invited to the baseball game? To grace the eggs-tra innings!

What makes a stew a rabbit stew? The presence of hares in it.

Why is a bunny's nose
not 12 inches long?
Because it wants a nose
not a foot!

Which region does the
Easter Bunny originally
come from? Albunny,
New York.

Why was Mr. Duck fired
from Easter service?
Because he kept
quacking the eggs.

Which kind of stories are the most preferred by bunnies? The ones with HOPpy ending.

Why is pork-chop love story legendary? Because it is a grill-deal.

What is the one potato mantra all potatoes live by? I think, therefore I ham.

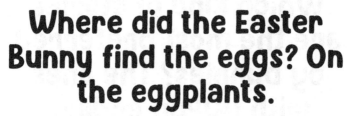

Where did the Easter Bunny find the eggs? On the eggplants.

What is a bunny from outer space called? Eggs-tra-terrestrial.

What made the Easter Bunny cross the road? The urge to prove that he wasn't chicken.

What is the quickest way to dry a bunny's hair? By using a hare dryer.

How do you get hot cross bunnies? By pouring boiling hot water down a rabbit hole.

What did the Easter bunny have to say about the Easter parade? That it was eggs-traordinary!

How do you know when a rabbit throws a tantrum? He is hopping mad!

What does a balding bunny have? A receding hareline.

Which bunny shies away from hopping? The chocolate one.

Which is the least favorite sport of the eggs? Running.

Which is Mr. Busy Bunny's favorite mode of travel? Hareplane.

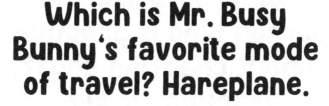

Why do bunnies feel lucky? Because they have four rabbit's feet at all times.

What is a bunny who keeps forgetting everything called? A hare brain.

What do you call a person who is practical about cracking eggs? Practical yolker.

How do you know the Easter Bunny is in a good mood? From his HOPpy expressions.

What do you call
dancing chicks? Poultry
in motion.

Where does Easter
occur before Valentine's
Day? In a dictionary.

Which seafood is most
popular on Easter? An
oyster bunny.

What do you say when you leave in between Easter lunch to attend a call? Eggs-cuse me.

What did Ms. Meow say to Mr. Bunny? That he had purr-fect eyesight.

What kinds of beans are found in the Easter garden? Jelly beans.

Who did the little eggs run away from at the Easter party? The egg-beater.

Why do you think carrots are good for the eyes? Because no bunny wears glasses.

Who is Mr. Bunny going to meet at the office? A Good Egg.

Knock! Knock! Who's there? Candy girl. Candy girl who? Can d girl have another piece of chocolate?

What's the name of the rabbit who stole from the rich and gave it to the poor? Rabbit Hood.

Which is the clumsiest candy bar? A Butterfinger!

Which room did the
Chocolate Couple book
for their honeymoon?
The two-bedroom
sweet.

What's invisible and
smells like carrots?
Rabbit farts.

What did Mrs. Bunny say
when she found a hare-
pin? This will definitely
come in candy.

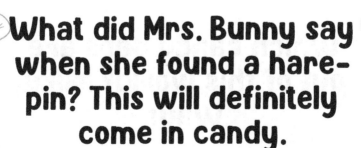

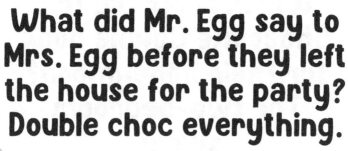

What did Mr. Egg say to Mrs. Egg before they left the house for the party? Double choc everything.

Which day is looked forward to by the bunnies all month? PayDay

Which candy bars are out of this world? Milky Ways

Which candies are from another planet? Mars Bars!

Why did Ms. Bunny quit her job? She was fed up with the hole thing.

Where does the Chocolate bunny note down all the important details? In his secret dairy.

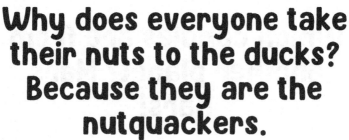

Why does everyone take their nuts to the ducks? Because they are the nutquackers.

Which season do ducks like the most? The fowl season.

What is the electrician's favorite ice cream flavour? Shock-a-lot.

What do you get when you dip a kitten in chocolate? A Kitty Kat bar.

How does an ant dipped in chocolate look? Decad-ant.

What is a French cat's favorite dessert? Chocolate mousse.

Why did the chocolate bar get angry? Because others called it nutty.

What did the bunny say to the duck? "You quack me up."

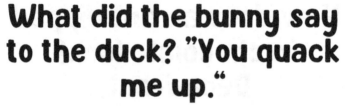

Why were the jelly beans studying too hard? They all wanted to be in the Smartie Bar Council.

Which is the most
popular soda on Easter?
Peepsi.

Why were the ducks
watching the news?
They wanted to see the
feather forecast.

Where did all the
candies on the plane go?
To visit the Sky-Bar.

What are chocolate coins for? They are mint to be eaten.

Where does the Doctor Rabbit work? At the hopspital.

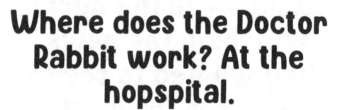

What did the bunny say when everyone complemented it regarding the new harestyle? "Thanks, but the credit goes to my haredressers."

What differentiates the Easter Bunny from the Comedian Bunny? The former is bunny and the latter is funny.

What looks like half a rabbit? The other half!

Why is a rabbit's tail not a ponytail? Because it's a bunny tail.

What is a Bunny Military
Commander called?
Napoleon Bunnyparte.

What kind of films do
ducks prefer?
Duckumentaries.

What is the name of the
global conference of
ducks? The World Wide
Web.

Why did Mr. Pig demand silence at home when he came back from office? Because he was in a choppy mood.

Which chocolate bunny is hard of hearing? The one whose ears are bitten off.

How are tough chicks born? From hard-boiled eggs.

What do ducks like at campfire nights? They like to witness campfire quackle at night.

 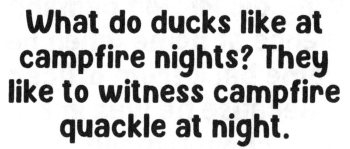

What is the similarity between a rabbit and a coin? Both have a head on one end and tail on the other.

How can you drop an egg six feet without breaking it? By dropping it seven feet as it would not break the first six feet.

Which is the state of origin of all the ducks? Dukota.

What is a rabbit in a kilt? Hopscotch.

What's common between a rabbit and an egg? Both run very fast as if they are unstoppable.

Which taco topping do ducks like the most? Quackamole.

What does Snow White like to have for breakfast? Egg whites.

"Where are the keys?," asked Mr. Bunny. "Did you chick in your pocket," answered Mrs. Buny.

What does a teacher
duck usually do to
punish her class? She
gives ducktation.

Why did the angry
rabbit skip his meal? He
didn't carrot at all.

Baby Fox asked Mother
Fox, "When should we
chase a rabbit?" "When
you fancy some fast
food," she answered.

What kind of a tree produces chicken? A poul-tree.

One film that the ducks cannot resist watching? The Lord of the Wings.

What is the name of the Detective Duck? James Pond.

What do you call a duck who got saved from a deadly accident? A lucky duck.

Why should you depend on haremail? Because of its quick delivery.

How did the egg climb the hill so high? By scrambling up!

Who do chicks visit when they fall sick? A ducktor.

What purpose did the long ears of rabbits serve? The ears covered their gray hares

Through which door did the eggs leave? The eggsit.

A duck who rules over a country with total power, control, and authority usually obtained by force is called? Ducktator.

Wat kind of eggs do comedians like? Funny side-up!

What did the chocolate say to the police? Can you hide me at a wafer place?

What is a bunny called
when it becomes too
rich? He is called a
millionhare.

How is the bunny's
videogame different
from yours? He presses
paws to play.

What happens to an egg
when it watches a
horror film? It gets
terri-fried.

What did the piglet say when it learned that the bunny ate all of its chocolates? How dairy!

What happens to Mother Hen if the temperature and humidity are high? She lays hard-boiled eggs.

What do ducks carry when they set out for a hike? A quackpack.

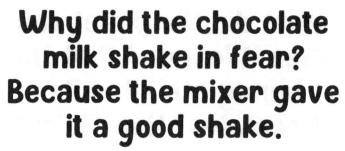

Why did the chocolate
milk shake in fear?
Because the mixer gave
it a good shake.

Which kind of chocolates
do pilots like on Easter?
Plane chocolates.

Why did the guy run
after the rabbit?
Because he loved the
chase.

What's different
between a bunny and
cold? You can catch the
latter, but not the
former.

What do you get when
you cross a rabbit and a
honey bee? A Bunny Bee.

Why is gold so precious
to bunnies? Because it
can be measured in
carrots.

What excuse did the bunny give to avoid the gym? He said he won't get fat as his food has no fat.

When do ducks wake up? At the quack of dawn.

What are bunny tales from their growing-up years called? Hare-raising tales.

What did the bunny say before disappearing the avocado? Avo-ca-dobra

What scares dust bunnies the most? Cleaning their hares.

What was the favorite beverage of choco bunny? Choco-latte.

Why did the bunny not go to the optician for his eye check-up? Because he went to Hoptician.

Why did the Easter Bunny bring toilet rolls? To save the scene from party poopers.

What is the one thing ducks always use to wrap Easter gifts? Duck tape.

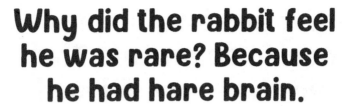

Why did the rabbit feel
he was rare? Because
he had hare brain.

What happens when a
frog is crossed with a
rabbit? A bunny ribbit.

What eggscuse did Ms.
Piggy have for putting
on so much weight? That
she had no time to
eggsercise.

Why are bunny holes so cool in summers? They are hare conditioned.

What do bunnies use to work online? Harenet.

What do health-conscious bunnies use to fry food? Hare-fryer

Made in United States
North Haven, CT
28 March 2024

50613508R00055